Wants You To
Know. . .

*You Are*
*Blessed*

Rae Simons

# Today God Wants You To Know. . .

## You Are Blessed

**BARBOUR BOOKS**
An Imprint of Barbour Publishing, Inc.

Scripture quotations marked KJV are taken from the King James Version of the Bible.

Scripture quotations marked NIV are taken from the HOLY BIBLE, NEW INTERNATIONAL VERSION®. NIV®. Copyright © 1973, 1978, 1984, 2011 by Biblica, Inc.™ Used by permission. All rights reserved worldwide.

Scripture quotations marked MSG are from *THE MESSAGE*. Copyright © by Eugene H. Peterson 1993, 1994, 1995, 1996, 2000, 2001, 2002. Used by permission of NavPress Publishing Group.

Scripture quotations marked NLT are taken from the *Holy Bible*. New Living Translation copyright© 1996, 2004, 2015 by Tyndale House Foundation. Used by permission of Tyndale House Publishers, Inc. Carol Stream, Illinois 60188. All rights reserved.

Scripture quotations marked NASB are taken from the New American Standard Bible, © 1960, 1962, 1963, 1968, 1971, 1972, 1973, 1975, 1977, 1995 by The Lockman Foundation. Used by permission.

Published by Barbour Books, an imprint of Barbour Publishing, Inc., 1810 Barbour Drive, Uhrichsville, Ohio 44683, www.barbourbooks.com

*Our mission is to inspire the world with the life-changing message of the Bible.*

Member of the
Evangelical Christian
Publishers Association

Printed in the United States of America.

# Contents

# *Introduction*

. . . . . . . . . . . . . . . . . . . . . . . . . . . . . . . . . . . .

*Blessed be the God and Father of our
Lord Jesus Christ, who has blessed us
with every spiritual blessing in the
heavenly places in Christ.*

EPHESIANS 1:3 NASB

Our lives are filled with God's blessings. Even our physical blessings have spiritual meaning. They come to us from "heavenly places."

In *Becoming the Beloved*, author Henri Nouwen writes that we need God's "ongoing blessing that allows us to hear in an ever-new way that we belong to a loving God who will never leave us alone but will remind us always that we are guided by love on every step of our lives."

So when we count our blessings, we're counting God's love letters, His reminders of His constant presence with us, His unconditional love. It's a message we can never hear too often. Luckily for us, it's also a message He never gets tired of sending!

# Part 1:
# WHAT IS A BLESSING?

## A Familiar Word?

*And God blessed them. . . .*
GENESIS 1:22 KJV

In the very first chapter of the first book of the Bible, we read that God was already in the business of blessing. He created the world—and then He blessed it. But what are we talking about when we use that familiar word *blessing*? Did you ever stop to think what it means to be blessed?

# Sixfold Blessings

. . . . . . . . . . . . . . . . . . . . . . . . . . . . .

*"I will be with you and bless you."*
GENESIS 26:3 NLT

*Merriam-Webster's Dictionary* gives six definitions for *bless*:

1. to hallow or consecrate
2. to invoke divine care for
3. to praise or glorify
4. to give happiness and prosperity
5. to protect and preserve
6. to endow or favor

God blesses you in all these ways. You are set aside to be God's dwelling place—and that makes you sacred. Through Christ, you have the right to ask God for help and care. He speaks to You; He gives You happiness and health; He protects you; and He gives you countless gifts!

# The Blessing Circle

- - - - - - - - - - - - - - - - - - - - - - - - - - - - - - - - - - - -

*May all. . .enter his circle of blessing*
*and bless the One who blessed them.*
PSALM 72:17 MSG

When we look at the Old Testament words translated as *bless* and *blessing*, we find deeper meanings. Two different Hebrew words are used in this psalm. The first one has to do with kneeling down; it's how we bless God. The second is how God blesses us; it means "to lead." These two blessings form a circle that never ends: God leads us, we surrender to God, He leads us even further. . .on and on.

## Fruitful Blessings

* * * * * * * * * * * * * * * * * * * * * * * * * * * * *

*"I will bless him, and will make him fruitful."*
GENESIS 17:20 NASB

The Hebrew word in this verse that we've translated as *bless* has to do with making something bear fruit. God blesses us by making our lives productive. We create homes and gardens, we raise children and help others; we write stories, paint pictures, and make music. That's one kind of fruitfulness He gives us. He also, however, makes our spirits bear a different kind of fruit—joy, humility, peace, understanding, and most of all, love.

# *Happiness!*

. . . . . . . . . . . . . . . . . . . . . . . . . . . . . . . . . . .

*How blessed is the one whom You
choose and bring near to You.*
PSALM 65:4 NASB

The Hebrew word used here simply means "happy."
When God chooses us, He makes us happy. When
He brings us near to Him, our hearts fill up with joy.
We'll still have the ups and downs that everyone else
has, of course. Sorrows will come, and we'll face days
that challenge us. But when we look back at our lives
as we enter eternity, we'll see clearly: we've been so
blessed. God's given us so much to make us happy!

# Spoken

. . . . . . . . . . . . . . . . . . . . . . . . . . . . . . . . . . . . .

*"Come, you who are blessed by my Father,*
*inherit the Kingdom prepared*
*for you from the creation of the world."*
MATTHEW 25:34 NLT

The Greek word translated as *blessed* in the New Testament adds another meaning to our understanding. In this verse, the word Jesus uses means "to speak well of, to say words that give or create something good." Speaking is important in the Bible. In Genesis, God spoke the world into being. Jesus is the Word. And your name is on God's lips. He has spoken your very self into being. You are a child of the Kingdom!

# The Blessing of True Identity

. . . . . . . . . . . . . . . . . . . . . . . . . . . . . . . . . .

*This is my beloved Son,*
*in whom I am well pleased.*
MATTHEW 17:5 KJV

This is the blessing the Father gave to Jesus at the beginning of His ministry. It's a spoken affirmation of a reality that already existed. Through grace, we can also claim this blessing as our own. When you feel down on yourself, when your self-esteem feels beaten down to nothing, repeat this blessing to yourself. It affirms your true identity. Christ has made you part of His family, and now you are God's beloved child. He is pleased with you!

# Consecrated

. . . . . . . . . . . . . . . . . . . . . . . . . . . . . . . . . . . .

*The cup of blessing which we bless, is it not*
*the communion of the blood of Christ?*
1 CORINTHIANS 10:16 KJV

The Greek word used here means "consecration;"
in other words, to commit something totally to God.
This adds another element to our understanding of
blessing: something that is blessed is completely
surrendered to God. We commune in our hearts with
Christ—we share intimately with Him in His absolute
self-giving on the cross—and this consecrates us. Our
hearts are God's. We have drunk from Christ's cup
of sacrifice and blessing.

# God's Abundance

. . . . . . . . . . . . . . . . . . . . . . . . . . . . . . . . . . . .

*God is able to bless you abundantly.*
2 CORINTHIANS 9:8 NIV

The literal meaning of these Greek words adds still another layer to our understanding of God's blessings. When Paul wrote this sentence to the Corinthians, he was talking about God's power—something that is over and above anything else we've ever encountered—to give grace and kindness to us that is also over and above anything we can even imagine. God's blessings are as abundant as His power to shower them upon us. None of our fears and doubts can ever limit either one!

# The Secret of Material Blessings

. . . . . . . . . . . . . . . . . . . . . . . . . . . . . . . . . . . . . .

*Be harmonious. . .kindhearted, and humble in spirit;*
*not returning evil for evil or insult for insult, but*
*giving a blessing instead; for you were called for*
*the very purpose that you might inherit a blessing.*
1 PETER 3:8–9 NASB

These verses contain two meanings of the Greek word for *blessing*: first, speaking well of others (this is one way we bless others, by affirming them with our words rather than gossiping, insulting, boasting, or quarreling); and second (the consequence of the first), tangible good things in our ordinary lives.

# Body and Soul

*Beloved, I pray that in all respects you may prosper and be in good health, just as your soul prospers.*
3 JOHN 1:2 NASB

The New Testament makes clear that God sends both physical and spiritual blessings into our lives. He wants our lives to be healthy and prosperous—emotionally, physically, financially, spiritually. We tend to separate the spiritual world from the physical one, but the Bible shows us a perspective where each sort of blessing flows into all the others. As we are spiritually blessed, our physical lives will be blessed as well.

Part 2:

# SPIRITUAL BLESSINGS

*Already Blessed*

*God. . .has blessed us in the
heavenly realms with every
spiritual blessing in Christ.*
EPHESIANS 1:3 NIV

That's pretty amazing. Right now, in the world of eternity—the spiritual world—you and I already possess all that God has to give to us. We don't have to wait for these blessings. We don't have to wait until we die and go to heaven. We don't have to earn them first, and we don't have to work hard to become "more spiritual." They're already ours, right now.

# Spiritually Strong

......................................................

*I long to see you so that I may
impart to you some spiritual
gift to make you strong.*
ROMANS 1:11 NIV

In this verse, Paul is talking about a particular kind of blessing: a spiritual gift. The Greek word is *charisma*, a grace-gift that empowers us to work on behalf of God's Kingdom. It's given to us freely; we don't have to do anything to earn it. We can't see this kind of blessing, but we can feel its power. It fills our lives with love, joy, and peace. We are spiritually strong. We have abundant life.

# *Thriving*

. . . . . . . . . . . . . . . . . . . . . . . . . . . . . . . . . . .

*I am like an olive tree, thriving
in the house of God. I will always
trust in God's unfailing love.*
PSALM 52:8 NLT

Children need love to thrive. So do all of us older folks. Without love, our hearts would be sad and lonely. Our lives would be narrow and unfulfilling. In fact, love is the most important of all the many spiritual blessings we've received. All God's blessings, both spiritual and physical, are wrapped up in His love. Because He loves us, He will never stop blessing us. His love never fails.

# The Ultimate Love

. . . . . . . . . . . . . . . . . . . . . . . . . . . . . . . . . . . . .

*This is how God showed his love among us:*
*He sent his one and only Son into the world*
*that we might live through him.*

1 JOHN 4:9 NIV

We don't have to try to grab hold of intangible proof of God's love. He sent it to us in the physical body of Jesus. Jesus was the love of God walking on earth. God blesses us in countless ways; He expresses His love through the many, many good things in our lives. But the ultimate expression of His love is still Jesus.

# Hearts Full of Love

. . . . . . . . . . . . . . . . . . . . . . . . . . . . . . . . . . . .

*God's love has been poured out into*
*our hearts through the Holy Spirit.*
ROMANS 5:5 NIV

God's love touches our entire lives. Even better, He pours His love into our very being. We are like a cup that God never stops filling up with His love. Love is a constant stream flowing into us until that love runs over and spills out to others. Because we have been blessed with God's unfailing love, we can pass that blessing on to others.

# *Reliable*

. . . . . . . . . . . . . . . . . . . . . . . . . . . . . . . . . . . . . . . . . . .

*We know and rely on the love*
*God has for us. God is love.*
1 JOHN 4:16 NIV

When we talk about God's love, it's not just a pretty phrase or some lofty theological concept. The Greek word translated here as *know* implies firsthand experience. We know God's love because it touches us personally. The more we allow ourselves to experience His love, the more we will be able to trust that love. We can put our full weight on it, knowing that God will never jerk it out from under us. How could He, when His very nature is love?

## Secure

. . . . . . . . . . . . . . . . . . . . . . . . . . . . . . . . . . .

*Such love has no fear, because perfect
love expels all fear. If we are afraid,
it is for fear of punishment.*
1 JOHN 4:18 NLT

Sometimes love hurts. Even the people who love us
most let us down—and we let them down. When we
say or do the wrong thing, they may pull back from
us. We fear we might lose their love. We worry they'll
leave us, even if it's only through death. But God's love
is perfect. It will never let us down. He never pulls away
from us, no matter what we do. We are totally secure.

# *For as Long as It Takes!*

. . . . . . . . . . . . . . . . . . . . . . . . . . . . . . . .

*Love is patient, love is kind. . .*
*bears all things, believes all things,*
*hopes all things, endures all things.*
1 CORINTHIANS 13:4, 7 NASB

We usually think of these verses as a description of how we should love others (which, of course, they are). But these familiar words also describe how God loves us. He is patient with us, no matter how many times we fall on our faces, no matter how long we take to learn something. He never stops believing in us. He's willing to put up with us for as long as it takes!

# At Home in the Love of Jesus

*"Just as the Father has loved Me,
I have also loved you; abide in My love."*
JOHN 15:9 NASB

Jesus loves you just as much as His heavenly Father loves Him. Think about it. The Son of God, the Word that existed before the beginning of the world, loves you infinitely, unconditionally, with all His heart. What a blessing! The only thing He asks in return is that you make His love your home—that you seek out the place where your heart is close to His.

# Relentless Love

. . . . . . . . . . . . . . . . . . . . . . . . . . . . . . . . . . . . . .

*I am convinced that nothing can ever separate us
from God's love. Neither death nor life, neither
angels nor demons, neither our fears for today nor
our worries about tomorrow—not even the powers
of hell can separate us from God's love.*
ROMANS 8:38 NLT

You can turn your eyes away from God. You can insist
on shutting your heart against Him. But God's love is
unstoppable and relentless. It leaks into the cracks of
your heart. It waits patiently for you to turn around
and notice it's there. It is always ready to bless you.

## Simply Love

* * * * * * * * * * * * * * * * * * * * * * * * * * * * * * *

*God is love, and all who live in love
live in God, and God lives in them.*
1 JOHN 4:16 NLT

We often make our spiritual lives so complicated. We focus on theology. We believe *our* church has got it right, and we worry about those folks in the church down the road who have got it all wrong. But the Bible says it's really quite simple: when we live in love, we are living in God. God is living in us. His blessing flows through us and out into the world.

# A Well of Joy

. . . . . . . . . . . . . . . . . . . . . . . . . . . . .

*When he arrived and saw this evidence of*
*God's blessing, he was filled with joy.*
ACTS 11:23 NLT

One of the spiritual blessings God gives us is joy—and all His other blessings increase that joy. Joy is like a spring of water that keeps spilling into our lives. Just when we think the spring has run dry, when we feel as though we'll never feel joy again, joy wells up. At first, it may just be a tiny trickle—but then it grows into a rushing stream that fills our hearts once more.

# God's House of Joy

............................................

*Strength and joy are
in his dwelling place.*
1 CHRONICLES 16:27 NIV

When we feel as though we're too weak to accomplish anything, we often feel blue and depressed. Our self-concepts suffer. We measure ourselves against others around us and come up lacking. But it doesn't have to be that way. When we stop focusing on our own lack and instead turn our eyes to God, He welcomes us with open arms into His house—a place where joy and strength go hand in hand.

## Strong Hearts

. . . . . . . . . . . . . . . . . . . . . . . . . . . . . . . . . . . . .

*"Don't be dejected and sad, for the
joy of the Lord is your strength!"*
NEHEMIAH 8:10 NLT

The Hebrew word used in this verse is *chedvah*,
meaning "rejoicing, gladness." Depression weakens
our hearts and separates us from others. But we have
a relationship with the Creator of the universe, and
He shares His eternal gladness with us. His joy makes
us strong, able to face the challenges of life, able to
reach out to others. Just as God shares His gladness
with us, we are meant to share our joy with everyone
we meet.

# Blessed with Laughter

........................................................

*You make known to me the path of life;*
*you will fill me with joy in your presence,*
*with eternal pleasures at your right hand.*
PSALM 16:11 NIV

Here, the Hebrew word is *samach*, which means joy in the sense of "mirth"—the sort of happiness that makes you laugh out loud. Our faith is not meant to be a gloomy, stern thing, filled with disapproval and a constant "No." Instead, those of us who follow Jesus say "Yes!" to life. We enjoy life! We smile and laugh a lot—because we know the pleasures God shows us will last throughout eternity.

# *Pursued by Joy*

. . . . . . . . . . . . . . . . . . . . . . . . . . . . . .

*Gladness and joy will overtake them,*
*and sorrow and sighing will flee away.*
ISAIAH 35:10 NIV

The Old Testament is filled with "joy words" that express different shades of meaning. In this verse, the Hebrew word *suws* contains within it the meanings of gladness, mirth, and rejoicing that we've already mentioned, but it has an added ingredient: "welcome." This is joy that runs after us with open arms. Even when we are deep in depression, wandering down dark and dreary paths, it catches up with us. Its presence—God's presence—chases away all our sadness.

# Springtime Joy

........................................................

*Shout for joy to the L*ORD*, all the earth,*
*burst into jubilant song.*
PSALM 98:4 NIV

This verse uses yet another Hebrew word: *patsach*,
which means "to make something burst open, to break
forth." It makes me think of a spring day, when green
buds are opening on every twig, and every bird and
frog is singing at the top of its lungs. God blesses
us with springtime joy, the sort of joy that can't be
contained. It breaks open our hard hearts, letting joy
and life spill out of us into the world.

*Abundant Goodness*

. . . . . . . . . . . . . . . . . . . . . . . . . . . . . . . . . . .

*Be glad in the L*ORD *and rejoice,*
*you righteous ones; and shout for joy,*
*all you who are upright in heart.*
PSALM 32:11 NASB

We often think of the Old Testament as being a bit gloomier than the New Testament—but look at all the verses that promise joy! Here our gladness is connected with the great bounty of blessings God has given to us. I'm reminded of a short verse by Robert Louis Stevenson: "The world is so full of a number of things, I'm sure we should all be as happy as kings." If we open our eyes, we'll see that God has filled our lives with abundant goodness.

# God in Action

················································

*When the righteous see God in*
*action, they'll laugh, they'll sing,*
*they'll laugh and sing for joy.*
PSALM 68:3 MSG

This Hebrew word for joy is *alats*, meaning "exults, rejoices in triumph." God is at work in our lives. His Spirit is moving and acting in amazing ways. What a blessing to know that the Creator of the world is working on our behalf, in a personal, intimate, ongoing way! How can we help but laugh and sing when we see Him triumph over the forces of darkness!

# Lift Up Your Voice!

. . . . . . . . . . . . . . . . . . . . . . . . . . . . . . . . . . . .

*They shall lift up their voice,*
*they shall sing for the majesty*
*of the LORD, they shall cry aloud.*
ISAIAH 24:14 KJV

There's a lot of singing going on in the Old Testament! Here the Hebrew word *ranan* refers to a happiness that's expressed vocally, with shouts of joy, with loud singing. Unfortunately, we haven't all been blessed with beautiful singing voices—but we *have* all been blessed by God in ways that make us sing! Even if we can't carry a tune, He's glad to hear our voices lifted up in praise.

# The Bridegroom

. . . . . . . . . . . . . . . . . . . . . . . . . . . . . . . .

*As a young man marries a young*
*woman, so will your Builder marry you;*
*as a bridegroom rejoices over his bride,*
*so will your God rejoice over you.*
ISAIAH 62:5 NIV

Imagine you're at a wedding. Now picture the way the groom looks at the bride as she walks down the aisle toward him. Can you see his look of total love and joy? His face tells everyone there how much he loves this woman, how glad he is to join his life with hers. That's how God loves *you*. You fill His heart with joy. He loves you so much that He wants to give Himself totally to you.

## Anointed with Joy

. . . . . . . . . . . . . . . . . . . . . . . . . . . . . . .

*"Your God has anointed you,*
*pouring out the oil of joy."*
HEBREWS 1:9 NLT

We find more promises of joy in the New Testament. The Greek word used here is *agalliao*, which contains within it the sense of both joyful welcome and exceeding gladness. It brings to mind the image of my mother's expression when I returned home for a Christmas gathering. As I came through the door, her face lit with such welcome as she hurried to give me whatever she could to make me happy. That's the sort of loving joy God pours over us!

## *Homecoming*

. . . . . . . . . . . . . . . . . . . . . . . . . . . . . . . . . . .

*Well done, thou good and
faithful servant. . .enter thou
into the joy of thy lord.*
MATTHEW 25:21 KJV

The word Jesus uses is *chairo*. It implies cheerfulness, a calm delight that's also closely connected to grace, God's undeserved, freely given blessings. We need to be careful not to get turned around in our understanding: the faithful servant didn't *earn* the Lord's joy with his hard work. Joy was simply the home that lay at the end of the road, the natural endpoint to his lifetime of service—a place of blessing and grace waiting for him to come home.

# Leap for Joy!

. . . . . . . . . . . . . . . . . . . . . . . . . . . . . .

*"Blessings await you when people hate you and exclude you and mock you and curse you as evil because you follow the Son of Man. When that happens, be happy! Yes, leap for joy!"*

LUKE 6:22–23 NLT

This is quite a promise! The word Jesus uses is *skirtaó*, which means literally "leap for joy." It's also the word used when a baby "quickens," when the mother first feels the movement of life. So Jesus is saying this: if you follow Him and feel misunderstood and separated from everyone around you—that's the very moment new joy will leap into life!

# Overflowing Joy

. . . . . . . . . . . . . . . . . . . . . . . . . . . . . . . . . . .

*I am exceeding joyful*
*in all our tribulation.*
2 CORINTHIANS 7:4 KJV

Paul confirms what Jesus already told His followers: in the midst of trouble, when no one understands us, when problems are everywhere we turn, we are blessed with joy! This joy isn't something small and weak, and it isn't merely a stiff-upper-lip endurance. Instead, the Greek word *chara* means joy that's abundant, overflowing—joy so great it can't even be measured. God's blessings are never limited by human problems—and He does nothing by half-measures!

## Inexpressible

. . . . . . . . . . . . . . . . . . . . . . . . . . . . . .

*You love him even though you have never*
*seen him. . . . You trust him; and you rejoice*
*with a glorious, inexpressible joy.*
1 PETER 1:8 NLT

From the world's perspective, it might seem as though Jesus is our imaginary friend. After all, we can't see Him, can't hear Him. But we know His presence is real because He has blessed us with a joy that lies beyond words. *Aneklálétos* is the word Peter uses here, a joy that's impossible to convey with words. It can't be grasped with language, can't be pinned down with any of our human concepts. But it's real!

# The Spiritual Blessing of Peace

. . . . . . . . . . . . . . . . . . . . . . . . . . . . . . . .

*"Peace I leave with you; My peace*
*I give to you. . . . Do not let your*
*heart be troubled, nor. . .fearful."*
JOHN 14:27 NASB

Jesus shares with us His own peace. Imagine that! We have access to the same peace of mind and heart He experienced during His life on earth. It's the legacy He left us, His going-away gift when He went back to His Father. "Don't *let* yourself be troubled," He tells us, indicating that we have a choice in the matter. All we have to do is accept this spiritual blessing He's shared with us.

# Peace Covenant

. . . . . . . . . . . . . . . . . . . . . . . . . . . . . . . . . . . . . .

*I give unto him my covenant of peace.*
NUMBERS 25:12 KJV

We humans make a lot of promises. We also break a lot of promises. Even when we start out with the best of intentions, we all too often find that we can't follow through with whatever we promised. God's promises are different from ours, though. When the Bible talks about a covenant, it's referring to a binding promise that can never be broken. God's promise of peace is a solid thing, firm and unchanging. It's a covenant that will never be broken.

# Peace in the Desert

. . . . . . . . . . . . . . . . . . . . . . . . . . . . . . . . . . . . . . . . . . .

*The LORD's justice will dwell in the desert,*
*his righteousness live in the fertile field.*
*The fruit of that righteousness will be peace. . .*
*quietness and confidence forever.*
ISAIAH 32:16–17 NIV

God's justice is simply the way He does things: fairly, without favoritism, ordering all things according to His own nature, creating peace and quiet confidence in our lives. The Hebrew word used here is *shalom*. It's more than freedom from conflict; it's also health and safety and completeness. It's ours not only in the midst of productive days like "fertile fields" but also in our empty "desert days."

# Forget Fear

. . . . . . . . . . . . . . . . . . . . . . . . . . . . . .

*"Go in peace. Your journey
has the LORD's approval."*
JUDGES 18:6 NIV

In this verse, shalom means "freedom from fear." We may not fear for our physical safety, but we often live with a constant, nagging anxiety, a sense that doom and gloom is hanging over us and the people we love. God wants to take that anxiety away from us. The word translated here as "approval" means literally "to go in front of." Knowing that God precedes us into the future, we can let go of all our worries. We can go in peace.

# Whole

. . . . . . . . . . . . . . . . . . . . . . . . . . . . . . . . . . . . . .

*And He said to her, "Daughter,*
*your faith has made you well;*
*go in peace and be healed."*
MARK 5:34 NASB

In the New Testament, instead of the Hebrew word *shalom*, we have the Greek word *eiréné*. Much like *shalom*, its meaning is far deeper than simply freedom from conflict. This peace means that all the essential parts of our lives are joined together. It means that we have been healed, body and soul. All the broken pieces of our hearts have been put back together. In Christ, we have been made whole.

# Guarded by Peace

*Then you will experience God's peace,*
*which exceeds anything we can understand.*
*His peace will guard your hearts and minds*
*as you live in Christ Jesus.*

PHILIPPIANS 4:7 NLT

We all crave peace. We long for that quiet sense that all is as it should be. It seems like too much to ask, though. After all, everyone has their share of troubles. But God's peace is deeper, wider, and greater than any peace we can imagine. We can't understand it—but we can experience it. It will guard our thoughts and emotions, even in the middle of heartache and trouble.

# Surrender

. . . . . . . . . . . . . . . . . . . . . . . . . . . . . .

*The mind governed by the*
*Spirit is life and peace.*
ROMANS 8:6 NIV

All through the Bible, God promises peace to His people. And yet our lives and our hearts are all too often shaken by conflict and fear. How can we access the peace that God promises? How can we experience it as something more than a fleeting emotion? The apostle Paul gives us the answer here: we need to surrender our thoughts to the Holy Spirit. This isn't easy. It takes discipline. In another verse, Paul calls it "taking every thought captive." But it's well worth the effort!

# Taught by God

. . . . . . . . . . . . . . . . . . . . . . . . . . . . . . . .

*I will instruct you and teach you in the*
*way which you should go; I will counsel*
*you with My eye upon you.*
PSALM 32:8 NASB

Another spiritual blessing that we're promised is God's guidance. This seldom means that we hear His voice speaking clearly, directly. He doesn't write His directions in big letters across the sky. Instead, He teaches us— and teaching is a process that's often long and slow. We have so much to learn, but God sees our lives clearly, and He has promised to teach us everything we need to know.

## Dawn

"The people living in darkness have seen
a great light; on those living in the land of
the shadow of death a light has dawned."

MATTHEW 4:16 NIV

We often feel as though we're stumbling around in the
dark. We'd like to follow God, but we're overwhelmed
by sorrows and discouragement. We don't know which
way to turn. But if we're patient, even the darkest
nights give way to the dawn. God's light will rise in our
lives once again—and all the shadows will disappear.

## *Spiritual Ears*

. . . . . . . . . . . . . . . . . . . . . . . . . . . . . . . . .

*Whether you turn to the right or to the left,*
*your ears will hear a voice behind you,*
*saying, "This is the way; walk in it."*
ISAIAH 30:21 NIV

Can you imagine how wonderful it would be if we could actually hear God's voice in our ears, whispering, "Go this way. Go that way. Now go *this* way." Maybe we depend too much on our five senses, though. We need to practice using our spiritual senses. If we want to hear God's voice, we need to listen with the ears of our spirits.

# God Knows Best

. . . . . . . . . . . . . . . . . . . . . . . . . . . . . . . . . . . . . . .

*This is what the LORD says—your Redeemer,*
*the Holy One of Israel: "I am the LORD your God,*
*who teaches you what is good for you and leads*
*you along the paths you should follow."*
ISAIAH 48:17 NLT

Sometimes we get in our heads that God likes to say no. We hesitate to ask for His direction because we're afraid He'll tell us we can't do something we want to do. But that's not the way God works. His guidance always is a yes to life, to health, to joy, to blessing.

# God's Word

........................................................

*Your word is a lamp to guide my*
*feet and a light for my path.*
PSALM 119:105 NLT

The Hebrew translation of *word* refers to any sort of communication. So how does God communicate with us? The obvious answer is through the Bible; scripture sheds light into our hearts and minds, helping us to see the right way to go. Christ is also called the Word, and He is the embodiment of God's communication with humans. As we study the life of Jesus in the Gospels, as we open our hearts to His Spirit, His light will guide us.

## *Heart Searching*

. . . . . . . . . . . . . . . . . . . . . . . . . . . . .

*Search me, O God, and know my heart;*
*try me and know my anxious thoughts;*
*and see if there be any hurtful way in me,*
*and lead me in the everlasting way.*
PSALM 139:23–24 NASB

Asking for divine guidance isn't like consulting a Magic 8 Ball. We don't get immediate answers. Instead, we need time alone with God, time when we open our hearts to Him. We have to be honest—with Him and with ourselves—willing to see our unhealthy thoughts and wrong behavior. Only then will He be able to bless us with His guidance.

# The Blessing of Insomnia!

*I will praise the LORD, who counsels me;*
*even at night my heart instructs me.*
PSALM 16:7 NIV

Do you ever lie awake, worrying? Do you sometimes dread those long, sleepless hours when everything looks darker than it does during the day? It doesn't have to be that way. Instead, whenever we have a bout of insomnia, we can use the time to open our hearts to God. If we surrender each worry to God, He can use this time to speak to our hearts.

# *Let There Be Light!*

. . . . . . . . . . . . . . . . . . . . . . . . . . . . . . . . . . . . .

*For God, who commanded the light to shine
out of darkness, hath shined in our hearts,
to give the light of the knowledge of the
glory of God in the face of Jesus Christ.*
2 CORINTHIANS 4:6 KJV

Humans have always loved light. Since the beginning of the twentieth century, starting with Einstein, physicists have been discovering amazing things about light that make it even more mysterious, even more wonderful. And God created it! If He could create light out of darkness and nothingness, He can shine the blessing of spiritual light into even the darkest hearts.

# Part 3:
# MATERIAL BLESSINGS

*Showered with Blessing*

> "I will bless my people and their
> homes. . . . And in the proper season
> I will send the showers they need.
> There will be showers of blessing."
> EZEKIEL 34:26 NLT

When we think of blessings, often what comes to mind are things like money, good health, a nice house, a car. God has nothing against those blessings—but He doesn't send them based on the power of positive thinking or the "law of attraction." Instead, when we let go of what we want, when we surrender everything to God, He showers us with exactly what we need.

## Blessed by Worship

. . . . . . . . . . . . . . . . . . . . . . . . . . . . . . . . . . . . . . . . .

*"Worship the LORD your God, and his*
*blessing will be on your food and water.*
*I will take away sickness from among you."*
EXODUS 23:25 NIV

The word translated as *worship* in this verse actually means "serve" or "work for," in the way that a farmer works the land or an employee works for her employer. It means serving God with our actions—and with our thoughts. When we do, He has promised to bless the food we eat and the water we drink. He will bless our bodies, and He will heal our hearts.

# Opened Floodgates

. . . . . . . . . . . . . . . . . . . . . . . . . . . . . . . . .

*"Test me in this," says the LORD Almighty,*
*"and see if I will not throw open the floodgates*
*of heaven and pour out so much blessing that*
*there will not be room enough to store it."*
MALACHI 3:10 NIV

The "law of attraction" says to think about what you want; focus your thoughts on it, and the Universe will give it to you. God tells us something different. He says surrender all your demands. Let go of all your ideas about what you need to be happy. When you do, He will pour more blessings into your life than you can even grasp.

## More Circles of Blessing

- - - - - - - - - - - - - - - - - - - - - - - - - - - - - -

*"The LORD your God. . .is giving
you power to make wealth."*
DEUTERONOMY 8:18 NASB

The Hebrew words used here are talking about wealth
and strength that are tied together. The meaning hints
at a well-equipped army that has all the supplies it
needs to be a powerful force. This works both ways:
God blesses us with strength that enables us to bring
good things into our lives—and we're made stronger
by the good things with which we've been blessed.
It's a blessing circle (the opposite of a vicious circle).

# First Things First

. . . . . . . . . . . . . . . . . . . . . . . . . . . . . .

*Those who seek the L*ORD
*lack no good thing.*
PSALM 34:10 NIV

The psalmist is reminding us again of what our priorities should be. We don't need to worry about material blessings. We don't need to focus our thoughts on them. Instead, we need to turn all our attention to the Lord. When we do, He will take care of our material needs. He will make sure we don't lack anything. When He is our priority, we can leave everything else up to Him.

# An Abundant God

. . . . . . . . . . . . . . . . . . . . . . . . . . . . . . . . . . . .

*The LORD will grant you*
*abundant prosperity.*
DEUTERONOMY 28:11 NIV

The Bible tells us again and again that God blesses abundantly, both spiritually and materially. Jesus' miracles embodied this aspect of God's nature. Look at the way He turned water into wine at the wedding in Cana, where the wine was better than anything that had yet been served. Think about when He fed the five thousand—and not only was there enough to go around, but there were leftovers. God will always bless us with more than enough!

# The Blessing Storehouse

*The LORD will open the heavens,
the storehouse of his bounty, to send
rain on your land in season and to
bless all the work of your hands.*
DEUTERONOMY 28:12 NIV

Most of us go to work every day in one form or another. We work in offices, schools, factories, and hospitals; in yards and homes; on farms, boats, and roadways. Some of us like our work. Some of us are doing the work only for the paycheck. Either way, God has promised to reach into the enormous warehouse where He keeps His blessings—and rain them down on our jobs.

# God's Pleasure

*Let them shout for joy, and be glad. . .*
*let them say continually, Let the LORD*
*be magnified, which hath pleasure in*
*the prosperity of his servant.*
PSALM 35:27 KJV

God's not stingy. He doesn't like to see us suffer. It makes Him happy to bless us with prosperity. When we truly believe we have a God who loves us like that, we can stop worrying so much about our bank accounts. Instead of stressing out every time we sit down to pay our bills, we can praise God, knowing it gives Him pleasure to supply what we need.

# God's Riches

.....................................

*God shall supply all your need according
to his riches in glory by Christ Jesus.*
PHILIPPIANS 4:19 KJV

Our material needs can seem overwhelming. We're
so aware of what we lack. Whether it's money or
physical strength, social skills or artistic talent, we're
more likely to feel poor than rich. We tend to feel that
we lack more than we have. But think about where
all our blessings come from—God's "riches in glory."
We can be certain that whatever we truly need, God
has more than enough to give us!

# Part 4

# BLESSINGS FROM NATURE

*God Revealed*

*For ever since the world was created, people have seen the earth and sky. Through everything God made, they can clearly see his invisible qualities— his eternal power and divine nature.*

ROMANS 1:20 NLT

The world of nature is another vehicle for God's blessings. The earth and the sky are filled with lovely and amazing things—enormous trees and tiny fern fronds; flaming sunsets and star-strewn skies; bird-song and whale song; summer thunderstorms and the intricacies of snowflakes. Each beautiful thing reveals God's wonder and power and loveliness.

# God's Metaphors

"God, who helps you. . .who blesses
you with blessings of the skies above,
blessings of the deep springs below."
GENESIS 49:25 NIV

The next time you look up at a blue, blue sky, remember that it is an expression of God's blessing. When you feel the sun on your face or moonlight pours through your window, think of God's light shining in your heart. When you see water spilling clear and bright out of the earth, remember that Jesus is a well of living water springing up within you.

*Lessons from Nature*

. . . . . . . . . . . . . . . . . . . . . . . . . . . . . . . .

*"But ask the animals what they think—let them
teach you; let the birds tell you what's going on.
Put your ear to the earth—learn the basics. Listen—
the fish in the ocean will tell you their stories. Isn't
it clear that they all know and agree that GOD is
sovereign, that he holds all things in his hand—
every living soul, yes, every breathing creature?"*
JOB 12:7–10 MSG

If we pay attention, we can learn a lot from nature.
The birds, the fish, the wild animals, the very soil itself,
all have stories to tell about God's blessings.

## God's Masterpieces

* * * * * * * * * * * * * * * * * * * * * * * * * * * * * *

*The LORD God made all sorts of trees grow up
from the ground—trees that were beautiful
and that produced delicious fruit.*
GENESIS 2:9 NLT

At the beginning of the Bible, in the book of Genesis, we learn that God created the natural world. Nature is His masterpiece, an endlessly beautiful expression of divine creativity. The many kinds of trees—pines and oaks, palms and willows, maples and tamarinds—are God's love poems. They speak to us of His unending power and love.

# Nature's Bounty

- - - - - - - - - - - - - - - - - - - - - - - - - - - - - - - -

*O Lord, how manifold are thy works!*
*in wisdom hast thou made them all:*
*the earth is full of thy riches.*
PSALM 104:24 KJV

The earth brims over with God's abundance: countless fish in the sea, thousands of species of flowers and butterflies and feathered creatures; trillions of tiny creatures too small for us to see; sunset after sunset and sunrise after sunrise; ocean and desert, forest and rivers. Everywhere we turn, we see beauty that tells us of the bountiful blessings of our Lord.

## Love That Never Fails

*The earth is full of his unfailing love.*
PSALM 33:5 NIV

Nature's beauty can take our breath away. Even in the midst of a city, nature's green life bursts out, and science has revealed to us still more of the mystery and wonder within the natural world. We humans often forget our vital connection to the rest of the earth, but we live in a beautiful world where each thing is dependent on everything else, a living, interconnected network that reveals God's love—a love that flows through the very structure of all life.

# *Wordless Praise*

. . . . . . . . . . . . . . . . . . . . . . . . . . . . . . . . . . . . . .

*The beast of the field shall honour me. . .*
*because I give waters in the wilderness,*
*and rivers in the desert.*
ISAIAH 43:20 KJV

Deer and woodchucks, chipmunks and rabbits, snakes and spiders, dragonflies and prairie dogs: each creature in its own way praises and honors God. Wordlessly, even without human intelligence and reasoning, they show us that God provides for His creation even in the most barren lands. His blessings reach into the wild, secret places. He forgets none of His creation and blesses it all.

# Heaven and Earth Are the Lord's

· · · · · · · · · · · · · · · · · · · · · · · · · · · · · · · · · · · · · · ·

*Behold, the heaven and the heaven
of heavens is the LORD's thy God,
the earth also, with all that therein is.*
DEUTERONOMY 10:14 KJV

Sometimes we forget that the earth is the Lord's. He has entrusted it to our care, but it is still His. When we exploit it, when we pollute the sky, when we pour poison into its waters, we are damaging something that belongs to God, not us. We are failing to honor and respect the great blessings He has given us through the natural world.

# Seeing the Lord in Nature

* * * * * * * * * * * * * * * * * * * * * * * * * * * * * * * * * * *

*The LORD wraps himself in light as with a garment;
he stretches out the heavens like a tent. . . . He
makes the clouds his chariot and rides on the wings
of the wind. He makes winds his messengers.*
PSALM 104:2–4 NIV

When you look up at the Milky Way sparkling across a night sky, you are seeing God's tent. Look at the sun streaming over the hills: you are seeing the Lord's garment. See the clouds that tower up in the sky before a storm: those are God's chariots. Listen to the wind blowing through the trees: you are hearing God's voice.

# Go with Joy

*For ye shall go out with joy, and be
led forth with peace: the mountains
and the hills shall break forth before
you into singing, and all the trees of
the field shall clap their hands.*

ISAIAH 55:12 KJV

The Bible tells us that humans and nature are connected. Another verse (Romans 8:22) speaks of the way in which the natural world groans and suffers because of sin. Here, the psalmist tells us that when we are set free to live in the Lord's joy and peace, the hills will hum a song of joy, and the trees will applaud. The earth is blessed when we are blessed.

## Wordless Sermons

. . . . . . . . . . . . . . . . . . . . . . . . . . . . . . . . . . .

*"Look at the birds of the air, that they do not
sow, nor reap nor gather into barns, and yet your
heavenly Father feeds them. Are you not worth
much more than they? . . . Observe how the lilies
of the field grow; they do not toil nor do they spin,
yet I say to you that not even Solomon in all his
glory clothed himself like one of these."*
MATTHEW 6:26, 28–29 NASB

If you're worried about your finances, spend some
time watching a robin—or looking at a flower. Both
of them have something to tell you.

*Tree of Life*

. . . . . . . . . . . . . . . . . . . . . . . . . . . . . . . . . .

*Jesus said, "How can I describe the Kingdom
of God? What story should I use to illustrate it?
It is like. . .the smallest of all seeds, but it
becomes the largest. . .it grows long branches,
and birds can make nests in its shade."*
MARK 4:30–32 NLT

When Jesus looked for something to help His followers
understand complicated ideas, He often turned to the
natural world. These symbols are still there around us;
every tree we look at can remind us we belong to a
Kingdom that grows in miraculous ways.

# *Worship*

"Worthy are You, our Lord and our God,
to receive glory and honor and power;
for You created all things, and because of
Your will they existed, and were created."
REVELATION 4:11 NASB

Enjoying the blessings of nature is also a form of worship. The awe and delight we feel when we see a towering mountain, a storm-tossed ocean, or a field of wildflowers can turn our hearts to God. When that happens, we're caught in another blessing circle: the more we worship God through nature's blessings, the more we are blessed!

# Part 5:
# BLESSINGS FROM
# OTHERS IN OUR LIVES

*Community of Believers*

*"For where two or three gather in
my name, there am I with them."*
MATTHEW 18:20 NIV

We all need time alone with God, but we also need
each other. Jesus and His followers taught that the
church—a community built on relationships—is God's
presence on earth. Together, we are the Body of
Christ. Together, we can bring hope and love to
those who are poor in spirit and body. And Jesus has
promised to be with us. Even if our "church" is only
two friends praying together, supporting each other
in the Lord's work, we bless one another.

# The Words of the Wise

*The words of the wise bring healing.*
PROVERBS 12:18 NLT

None of us knows everything. No matter how mature we are in Christ, we all have times when our own knowledge runs out. We find ourselves confused, overwhelmed, weak. In times like those, we need friends and teachers, counselors and pastors who can share their wisdom with us. We need to be humble enough to ask for help—and then we need to be willing to open our minds and hearts to the healing we need.

## The Blessing of True Love

. . . . . . . . . . . . . . . . . . . . . . . . . . . . . . . . .

*Love never gives up. Love cares more for others
than for self. Love doesn't want what it doesn't
have. Love doesn't strut, doesn't have a swelled
head, doesn't force itself on others, isn't always "me
first," doesn't fly off the handle, doesn't keep score
of the sins of others, doesn't revel when others
grovel, takes pleasure in the flowering of truth,
puts up with anything. . .always looks for the best,
never looks back, but keeps going to the end.*
1 CORINTHIANS 13:4–7 MSG

How blessed we are when others love us like that!

# *The Kiss of Peace*

*Love and faithfulness meet together;*
*righteousness and peace kiss each other.*
PSALM 85:10 NIV

The New Testament has a lot to say about the way God blesses us through our relationships with others—but so does the Old Testament. The psalmist tells us that love and faith go hand in hand. Living in peace with others is the road to righteousness. Here's another of those blessing circles! God blesses us when we live out our faith by loving others—and when we treat others with love, making an effort to resolve disagreements, our faith is strengthened.

# The Blessing of Friendship

*A friend loves at all times,*
*and a brother is born for adversity.*
PROVERBS 17:17 NASB

When things are going our way, we may be tempted to think we are so strong that we don't need anyone's help. We may consider ourselves so spiritually mature that we can go it alone, "just me and the Lord." But sooner or later, all of us face times when everything seems to fall apart. We can't cope with life, and even our faith falters. When a friend quietly offers us her hand, that's the moment when we truly understand the blessing of friendship!

# Painful Blessings

As iron sharpens iron,
so a friend sharpens a friend.
PROVERBS 27:17 NLT

Our friends can bring out the best in us. Sometimes that's a pleasant experience. We bask in the knowledge that someone truly understands and appreciates us. But a real friend doesn't only stroke our egos. He also speaks the truth to us, even when it's difficult for us to hear. He hones us, the way a knife is made sharper and more useful by being rubbed against another knife. And sometimes that can be painful!

# Heartfelt Blessings

*The pleasantness of a friend springs
from their heartfelt advice.*
PROVERBS 27:9 NIV

Down through the years, God uses our friends to bless us again and again. We feel joy in their company, laughing and having fun together. In times of sorrow and discouragement, we are comforted by their love and faith in us. Their prayers strengthen us. And most of all, we benefit from their wisdom. God has taught each of us unique insights, and we are blessed when our friends share with us their hearts' wisdom.

# Entertaining Angels

*Do not neglect to show hospitality
to strangers, for by this some have
entertained angels without knowing it.*

HEBREWS 13:2 NASB

In the New Testament, the Greek word translated as *hospitality* literally means "love of strangers"—and the word for *angel* means "messenger." The author of Hebrews is telling us that it's not only our friends who bless us. Sometimes God sends strangers into our lives with a message we need to hear. Are our hearts open when we meet someone who seems different from us? Are we willing to hear God speaking through that person?

## Blessed by the Stranger

. . . . . . . . . . . . . . . . . . . . . . . . . . . . . . . . . . . . . . . . . .

*"For I was hungry and you gave me something*
*to eat, I was thirsty and you gave me something*
*to drink, I was a stranger and you invited me in. . .*
*I was sick and you looked after me, I was in*
*prison and you came to visit me. . . . Truly I tell*
*you, whatever you did. . .you did for me."*
MATTHEW 25:35–36, 40 NIV

Strangers aren't only angels in disguise! They're also Jesus Himself. When we give to others in need, we are giving to our Lord.

# Blessed by Those in Need

. . . . . . . . . . . . . . . . . . . . . . . . . . . . . . . .

*"When you give a banquet,*
*invite the poor, the crippled, the lame,*
*the blind, and you will be blessed."*
LUKE 14:13–14 NIV

When we give to those in need, we may think we are the ones who are doing God's work. And we are, of course; God is using us to bless others. But at the same time, we may find that we're the ones who are blessed the most. Not only will God bless us, but we'll also find that the poor, the sick, the stranger, and the prisoner all have blessings to give us.

# Don't Forget to Say Thank You

*I always thank my God for you.*
1 CORINTHIANS 1:4 NLT

When you thank God for the many blessings He has given you, don't forget the people He has put in your life. Thank Him for your friends and your family, your coworkers and your employers. Thank Him for the people you know casually and for each stranger you pass on the street. Thank Him even for the difficult people you encounter! Each and every one of them can be a vehicle for God's blessing to flow into your life.

# Part 6:
# BLESSINGS IN THE
# MIDST OF TROUBLE

*Blessed in the Presence*
*of My Enemy*

*You prepare a feast for me in the presence of my enemies. . . . My cup overflows with blessings.*
PSALM 23:5 NLT

We often think of blessings as things we experience in the happy times. When we get a raise, when we are healed from some illness, or when our children and our elderly parents are all happy and healthy, we consider that we've been blessed. But the psalmist reminds us that God blesses even when enemies surround us. God's blessings are just as bountiful on dark days as they are on sunny days.

# Blessed When
# We Are Broken

The LORD is close to the brokenhearted;
he rescues those whose spirits are crushed.
PSALM 34:18 NLT

The meanings found in this verse's Hebrew words are rich with blessings: When we've been broken, crushed by life, hurt so badly that we feel we can't survive, the Self-Existent Eternal One is as intimate with us as a close friend, as close by as if He were sitting at our side. When our inner beings are ground down to nothing, He sets us free, He helps us, and He makes us safe. He opens wide all the doors in our lives.

# Speed-of-Light Blessings

*God is our refuge and strength,*
*an ever-present help in trouble.*
PSALM 46:1 NIV

The Hebrew word that's been translated as *ever-present* is an interesting one. It carries within it several meanings: something that's diligent and never gives up; something unbelievably fast; something that shouts louder than any other sound. That's the way God's blessings reach us when we're in trouble—unstoppable, breaking the sound barrier, faster than the speed of light. No matter how big the problem, His help will be there when we need it.

# The Blessing of Weakness

*I will boast all the more gladly
about my weaknesses, so that
Christ's power may rest on me. . . .
I delight in weaknesses, in insults,
in hardships, in persecutions,
in difficulties. For when I am weak,
then I am strong.*

2 CORINTHIANS 12:9–10 NIV

People don't very often say, "God has blessed me richly by making me so weak." No, we usually think of strength as a blessing—and weakness is more like a curse! But that's not what Paul says here. In the midst of weakness, hardship, and difficulties, he says, we are blessed with God's power.

# *Rejoicing in Times of Trial*

*We can rejoice, too, when we run into
problems and trials, for we know
that they help us develop endurance.
And endurance develops strength of
character, and character strengthens
our confident hope of salvation. And this
hope will not lead to disappointment.
For we know how dearly God loves us.*

ROMANS 5:3–5 NLT

In this verse, Paul has more to say about the blessings
we can find during times of trouble. He spells out what
some of them are: endurance, strength of character,
hope—and most of all, the confidence that God
loves us.

## The Blessing of Confidence

*Though a mighty army surrounds me,*
*my heart will not be afraid. Even if I*
*am attacked, I will remain confident.*
PSALM 27:3 NLT

Confidence is truly one of the blessings we can gain from the hard times we face. It doesn't come to us immediately, but with each challenge we face, we grow more certain of God's power to overcome even the greatest problems. We remember that He did it before—and we can begin to trust that He will do it again. God is bigger than any enemy we face!

# God's Castle of Blessing

*The LORD also will be a refuge for the oppressed, a refuge in times of trouble.*
PSALM 9:9 KJV

The Hebrew word translated "refuge" is *sagab*—a stronghold on a high mountain or cliff. Why is the refuge situated like this? Because a stronghold on a mountain or cliff has a good view of any enemies that might approach—and it can be defended more easily if it's attacked. Picture one of those enormous storybook castles in the mountains of Germany, all the towers and the strong wall around the entire thing. That's the sort of refuge God offers us in times of trouble!

*Blessings during*
*Times of Drought*

. . . . . . . . . . . . . . . . . . . . . . . . . . . . . . . . . . . .

*"Blessed is the man who trusts. . .*GOD, *the woman who sticks with* GOD. *They're like trees replanted in Eden, putting down roots near the rivers—never a worry through the hottest of summers, never dropping a leaf, serene and calm through droughts, bearing fresh fruit every season."*
JEREMIAH 17:7–8 MSG

God never promises us that troubles won't come into our lives. What He does promise is that no matter how dry and empty our external lives are, He will supply our hearts with the blessing of life. We don't need to worry!

# One Foot in Front of Another

. . . . . . . . . . . . . . . . . . . . . . . . . . . . . . . . . . . .

*God blesses those who patiently endure
testing and temptation. Afterward they
will receive the crown of life that God
has promised to those who love him.*

JAMES 1:12 NLT

It's not easy to feel blessed during hard times. Our emotions tell us that everything is *awful*. But we need patience. The Hebrew word used here has to do with perseverance. That means just putting one foot in front of the other for as long as it takes. That's all God asks of us while He supplies the blessings, both now and in eternity.

## Being Honest with God

. . . . . . . . . . . . . . . . . . . . . . . . . . . . . . . . . . .

*O LORD, why do you stand so far away?*
*Why do you hide when I am in trouble?*
PSALM 10:1 NLT

All of us have experienced the feeling the psalmist describes here. No matter how many verses we read about blessings in the midst of trouble, we don't *feel* blessed. Jesus felt the same way when He hung on the cross—and like the psalmist, He wasn't afraid to express His feelings to His Father. Sometimes bitterness, discouragement, and anger are all we have to offer God. We can be honest with God. He accepts and blesses even our negative emotions.

## Songs of Deliverance

......................................................

*You are my hiding place; You preserve
me from trouble; You surround me
with songs of deliverance.*
PSALM 32:7 NASB

When our hearts are full of doubt and despair, how can we experience God's blessings? Sometimes, we just have to endure our emotions with that one-foot-in-front-of-the-other patience we mentioned earlier. But we do have options, even then. Prayer, scripture, the support of others, and even music can become "hiding places" where we can escape, even temporarily, and experience God's presence.

# The Blessing of Scripture

. . . . . . . . . . . . . . . . . . . . . . . . . . . . . . . . .

*Those who hope in the LORD will renew their strength. They will soar on wings like eagles; they will run and not grow weary, they will walk and not be faint.*

ISAIAH 40:31 NIV

Scripture verses like this are good to read over and over during hard times. Write them on note cards and tape them to your car's dashboard or your computer monitor—wherever your eyes go regularly throughout the day. The more you read them, the more they will come to life. . .the more you will believe you are blessed.

# Gentle Jesus

* * * * * * * * * * * * * * * * * * * * * * * * * * * * * * * * * *

*Jesus said, "Come to me, all of you
who are weary and carry heavy burdens,
and I will give you rest. . . . Let me teach you,
because I am humble and gentle at heart,
and you will find rest for your souls."*
MATTHEW 11:28–29 NLT

Jesus longs to lift our burdens from our shoulders.
Like a mother worrying over her child, He yearns to
do whatever He can to ease our troubled hearts. He
knows how hard it is for us—and He'll take the time
to teach us all we need to know to trust Him.

## *Following God in the Darkness*

* * * * * * * * * * * * * * * * * * * * * * * * * * * *

*"Be strong and courageous! Do not be afraid
and do not panic. . .for the LORD your God will
personally go ahead of you. He will neither
fail you nor abandon you."*

DEUTERONOMY 31:6 NLT

Feeling sad and discouraged is one thing. Panicking
is another. Panicked people have stopped thinking.
They've relinquished all control, and they've let fear
take the driver's seat. We can't always control negative
emotions—but we can refuse to let fear drive all sense
from our heads. Instead, we can cling to the thought
that God's presence is going ahead of us into the
darkness.

# Renewed Hope

*I cried out, "I am slipping!" but your unfailing love,
O Lord, supported me. When doubts filled my mind,
your comfort gave me renewed hope and cheer.*
PSALM 94:18–19 NLT

This verse always makes me think of the Gospel story where Peter is walking on the water—and suddenly starts to sink beneath the waves because he's taken his eyes off Jesus and begun to doubt (Matthew 14). "Lord, save me!" Peter shouts. And Jesus doesn't scold him for his doubt. Instead, the scripture says, "Immediately Jesus reached out his hand and caught him" (Matthew 14:31 NIV).

## *Mother Love*

. . . . . . . . . . . . . . . . . . . . . . . . . . . . . . . . . . . . . .

*"As a mother comforts her child,
so will I comfort you."*
ISAIAH 66:13 NIV

Whether we are mothers ourselves, have had a loving mother, or have had a woman in our lives who has loved us like a mother, most of us know that a mother's love is the sort that doesn't ask questions before it rushes to help. If her children are in danger, a mother will do whatever she has to in order to save them. In good times and bad, her whole identity is focused on blessing her children. Remember—that's the way God loves you!

# Resurrection Blessings

· · · · · · · · · · · · · · · · · · · · · · · · · · · · · · · · ·

*We are hard pressed on every side, but not crushed; perplexed, but not in despair; persecuted, but not abandoned; struck down, but not destroyed. We always carry around in our body the death of Jesus, so that the life of Jesus may also be revealed in our body.*
2 CORINTHIANS 4:8–10 NIV

Paul's decision to follow Jesus didn't bring him the easy life. Instead, he faced prison, shipwreck, and misunderstanding. He could have given up; he could have thrown up his hands and said, "What's the use?" Instead, he identified with Jesus, knowing that in Him, new life always follows death.

# *The God of All Grace*

. . . . . . . . . . . . . . . . . . . . . . . . . . . . .

*Therefore humble yourselves under the mighty
hand of God, that He may exalt you at the proper
time, casting all your anxiety on Him, because He
cares for you. . . . After you have suffered for a little
while, the God of all grace. . .will Himself perfect,
confirm, strengthen and establish you.*
1 PETER 5:6–7, 10 NASB

Here's a summary of how we can experience God's
blessings in the midst of trouble: with humility (not
insisting on our own way), with patience (putting one
foot in front of another), and with trust (giving all our
anxiety to God).

# Part 7:
# BLESSINGS ON OUR FAMILIES, HOMES, AND WORK

## Blessings for Your House

*"Put your entire trust in the Master Jesus. Then you'll live as you were meant to live— and everyone in your house included!"*
ACTS 16:31 MSG

God's blessings are not just for us. When we trust Jesus, our lives find a healthy balance. Blessings flow out around us, into our families, our homes, and our workplaces. As we surrender to God all the people and things that concern us most, we will see Him pour out His love and grace.

# *The Voice of Experience*

. . . . . . . . . . . . . . . . . . . . . . . . . . . . . . . . . . . .

*I was young and now I am old, yet I have never seen
the righteous forsaken or their children begging
bread. They are always generous and lend freely;
their children will be a blessing.*
PSALM 37:25–26 NIV

These are worrisome days. We worry about our jobs
and the economy. We worry about what the world
will be like by the time our children are entering the
work world. We worry about our retirement. But the
psalmist tells us we don't need to worry. We can trust
that we and our children will be blessed with enough
to bless others.

# *It's Up to You!*

I place before you Life and Death,
Blessing and Curse. Choose life so
that you and your children will live.
DEUTERONOMY 30:19 MSG

We may feel as though we're at the mercy of fate. Some of us are lucky, some of us are unlucky, and there's nothing we can do about it. But God says that's not how things work. Instead, we each have a choice to make. When we choose life, we will find blessings everywhere we turn. But if we choose death, we will see only curses in the same circumstances. Which do we want for our children?

# Trusting God with Our Children

. . . . . . . . . . . . . . . . . . . . . . . . . . . . . . . . . . . . .

*"For I will fight those who fight you,
and I will save your children."*

ISAIAH 49:25 NLT

Until I had children, I didn't worry much. News of wars and accidents, illnesses and disasters didn't make me turn cold with fear. I got on planes without being anxious they might crash, and I wandered fearlessly through city streets. Once I had children, though, the world was full of dangers. For the first time, I learned what it really meant to trust God. I had to accept that I couldn't keep my children safe—but He could, all the way into eternity.

## Divine Education

. . . . . . . . . . . . . . . . . . . . . . . . . . . . . . . . . . .

*"All your children will be taught by the Lord,*
*and great will be their peace."*
Isaiah 54:13 niv

Whether or not we have our own children, most of us have children we love. As much as we love them—and we really do!—we all, if we're honest, know that in one way or another we've let these children down. So it's good to know that God will fill in the gaps we've left in our children's education. As we surrender to God both our love for them and the mistakes we've made, God will bless them with His peace.

## *Coming Home Again*

. . . . . . . . . . . . . . . . . . . . . . . . . . . . . . . . . . .

*"Your children will come back to you
from the distant land of the enemy."*
JEREMIAH 31:16 NLT

Teenagers can be a challenge. Adolescents are struggling hard to find their identities. In the process, they often refuse to be anything like the adults who love them. That's healthy, a part of growing up—but their rejection of our deepest beliefs can be both painful and terrifying. Once again, God asks us to surrender these children into His hands, in newer ways than ever before. He will go with them where we can't go, and He will bring them back again. His blessings never cease.

# Jesus Loves the Little Children

. . . . . . . . . . . . . . . . . . . . . . . . . . . . . . . . . . . . . . .

*Then he took the children in*
*his arms and placed his hands*
*on their heads and blessed them.*
MARK 10:16 NLT

The Gospels show us that Jesus loved children. He expressed His love to the children around Him much the same as we do to our children: with hugs and pats and kind words. He affirmed them and let them know they were important. He blessed them. Jesus is no longer walking our earth, calling children to Him for physical hugs. But He hasn't stopped blessing children. He never will.

# Long-Term Blessings

"So there is hope for your descendants,"
declares the LORD. "Your children will
return to their own land."
JEREMIAH 31:17 NIV

We are often shortsighted, but God always takes the long perspective. He not only looks into the future; He also is building it right now. At this very moment, He is blessing you in ways that will one day bless your children and their children and *their* children. His blessings flow down through the generations. We may look at the present moment and feel discouraged—but God does long-term work.

# A Thousand Generations

. . . . . . . . . . . . . . . . . . . . . . . . . . . . . . . . .

*"Know therefore that the LORD your God, He is God,*
*the faithful God, who keeps His covenant and His*
*lovingkindness to a thousandth generation."*
DEUTERONOMY 7:9 NASB

Most of us worry about our children. We may also worry about our grandchildren and even our great-grandchildren. God says He will be faithful not only to them but also to a thousand generations into the future. That's hard to comprehend—but remember, you are here today because God was also with the thousand generations that came before you. He's not going to fail your children or grandchildren. . .or great-great-great-grandchildren!

# God's Promise to Our Children

*"I will pour out my Spirit on
your descendants, and my
blessing on your children."*
ISAIAH 44:3 NLT

We'd like to give so many things to the children we
love: health. . .safety. . .happiness. . .security. Most
of all, we wish we could send our love with them
wherever they go throughout their entire lives. We
long to wrap them up forever in our arms the way
we could when they were small. We can't, of course.
That's one of the hard lessons of parenthood. But
God's Spirit will do what we can't.

# Home Sweet Home

*My people shall dwell in a peaceable habitation, and in sure dwellings, and in quiet resting places.*
ISAIAH 32:18 KJV

God has also promised to bless our homes. He's not talking about a vague, "spiritual" blessing that's hard to truly grasp. He's promising us something concrete that exists in the real world: a home where we can feel safe, where we can rest and be quiet. So the next time you look around your house and see worn carpets, clutter, or smudgy windows, remember that your home is blessed by God—and He lives there with you!

# Paid in Full

. . . . . . . . . . . . . . . . . . . . . . . . . . . . . . . . . . .

*Do your best. Work from the
heart for your real Master,
for God, confident that you'll
get paid in full when you
come into your inheritance.*
COLOSSIANS 3:24 MSG

Paul understood how frustrating it can be to work hard and get paid little, to feel as though no one is appreciating your full effort and skill. In this verse, he reminds us again: no matter what our job or profession, we work for Christ. Even on those days when we hate our jobs—and we all have at least a few of those days!—He will bless our efforts.

# The Work of Righteousness

*And the work of righteousness will be peace, and the service of righteousness, quietness and confidence forever.*
ISAIAH 32:17 NASB

What if every day when we started our work, we remembered that we're serving God and His Kingdom? What if instead of obsessing about success or failure, our paycheck or a promotion, or any other earthly goal, we focused all our hearts and minds on building the Kingdom of God? If we did that, this verse promises, we'll be blessed with peace—a quiet and eternal confidence that we are doing the work God needs us to be doing.

# Embrace Life!

. . . . . . . . . . . . . . . . . . . . . . . . . . . . . . . . . . . .

*Take your everyday, ordinary life—*
*your sleeping, eating, going-to-work,*
*and walking-around life—and place*
*it before God as an offering.*
*Embracing what God does for you*
*is the best thing you can do.*
ROMANS 12:1 MSG

Our attitudes shape our emotions. They also shape what we see in the world around us. If we look at the world with angry, suspicious eyes, we see slights and insults everywhere we turn. But if we look at each aspect of our lives as an offering to God, we will find blessings instead of curses. When we open our hearts and embrace life, we are blessed.

# Part 8:
# THE BLESSING OF GOD'S PRESENCE

*The Greatest Blessing*

*Praise the Lord; praise God our savior!*
*For each day he carries us in his arms.*
PSALM 68:19 NLT

When we count our blessings, we usually list the good things in our lives. We may remember to include spiritual blessings like peace and joy and a sense of the Lord's leading. But do we remember the greatest blessing of all? God—the Creator of the universe—is present with us every minute of every day! What greater blessing could there possibly be than that?

# Inner Treasure

........................................

*We now have this light shining in our hearts,*
*but we ourselves are like fragile clay jars*
*containing this great treasure.*
2 Corinthians 4:7 NLT

God is not only present in the world around us; He is also present in our hearts, in our inner beings. Imagine that! The same God who made the stars, who keeps our sun burning and our earth turning around the sun, who waters and nourishes all the life on our planet— that God lives inside you. You carry treasure within your very being.

## All I Want

"You are my place of refuge.
You are all I really want in life."
PSALM 142:5 NLT

Earlier, we spoke of the refuge God offers us in trouble, the blessings that come to us even in the midst of sorrow and hardship. In this verse, the psalmist reminds us that in good times *and* bad, God Himself is our safe place. When we believe He is the only thing we truly need, we no longer have to worry about death and loss and failure. We can rest in the knowledge that we are blessed with His presence—no matter what.

# The Shelter of God's Love

. . . . . . . . . . . . . . . . . . . . . . . . . . . . . . . . . . . . . . .

*In the shelter of your presence. . .*
*you keep them safe. . .*
*from accusing tongues.*
PSALM 31:20 NIV

We all worry about what other people think of us. We want people to like us. We want them to approve of us. We want to impress them. When we succeed in doing all that, we feel good about ourselves—but when we don't, we often feel less worthy, full of despair and self-doubt. We don't have to live like that. Instead, we can live in the shelter of God's presence, knowing that His love is always with us.

# Normal Life

. . . . . . . . . . . . . . . . . . . . . . . . . . . . . . . . . . .

*"My Presence will go with you,*
*and I will give you rest."*
EXODUS 33:14 NIV

Sometimes life seems so *hard*. We face one challenge after another: sickness, problems with our parents or our children, financial worries, car trouble, broken relationships. We say to ourselves, "When will life get back to *normal*?"—but it never does. Finally, we have to accept that these endless challenges *are* normal life, so we'll need to look somewhere else for relief. When we turn to God, we find His presence already there, offering us rest even in the midst of all life's challenges.

## God's Contagious Joy

*You will fill me with joy in your presence,*
*with eternal pleasures at your right hand.*

PSALM 16:11 NIV

Life isn't *all* hard! God longs to share with us His own joy. Think about how easy it is to catch a good mood from your spouse or a close friend. It's the same with God. His presence is never sad or gloomy. It's not disapproving and stern. His joy is greater than any human's. When we spend time in His presence, we catch His joy. We find pleasures that will last throughout all eternity.

# Screaming God's Name

. . . . . . . . . . . . . . . . . . . . . . . . . . . . . . . . . .

*The LORD is near to all
who call upon Him.*
PSALM 145:18 NASB

The Hebrew word that's translated as *call* in this verse doesn't mean that we're calling God the way we call a dog. It's not the same thing as calling a friend on the phone. Instead, the word is a lot stronger. It means to scream God's name out loud so that everyone around us can hear. It's an affirmation of our faith in God's very identity. God's presence is already there with us—but a call like that changes our own hearts so that we finally *know* He's there.

# The Angel of God's Presence

*The angel of His*
*presence saved them.*
ISAIAH 63:9 NASB

God is always with us. He understands how limited our perceptions are, though, so sometimes He sends "angels" into our lives whom we can touch with our hands, hear and see with our physical ears and eyes. The Hebrew word used here is *malak*: a messenger, an ambassador, an envoy. Our lives are full of people who can make real to us the presence of God. They carry His messages. We just need to listen.

# Stop Being Afraid!

. . . . . . . . . . . . . . . . . . . . . . . . . . . . . . . . . . .

*"Be strong and courageous! Do not be afraid or discouraged. For the LORD your God is with you wherever you go."*
JOSHUA 1:9 NLT

The Bible is constantly telling us not to be afraid. There are at least 145 verses that communicate that message in one form or another, as though God is trying very hard to get the meaning across: *I AM with you. Why are you so worried? Please trust Me!* He is patient with our fear—but He longs to take it from us.

## Remain in Jesus

· · · · · · · · · · · · · · · · · · · · · · · · · · · · · ·

*"If you remain in me and I in you,*
*you will bear much fruit;*
*apart from me you can do nothing."*

JOHN 15:5 NIV

Many of us believe independence is a good thing. We feel we should be able to "go it alone," that we should be strong enough to "stand on our own two feet." Jesus wants us to look at things differently. He wants us to open our tight grip on our lives and instead take His hand. He knows that only then will we be able to live truly productive lives, lives that are blessed with spiritual and physical blessings.

## Lovingkindness

· · · · · · · · · · · · · · · · · · · · · · · · · · · · · · · · · · · ·

*Yet the LORD will command his lovingkindness in
the day time, and in the night his song shall be
with me, and my prayer unto the God of my life.*
PSALM 42:8 KJV

Think of it—God is with you each moment of the day!
He's in the car or on the bus with you as you go to
work or run errands. He sits at the table with you while
you eat. He never leaves you; His love and kindness
are always right there beside you. And at night, when
you go to bed, He's singing you His lullaby.

# Pilgrims

............................................

*Blessed are those whose strength is in you,*
*whose hearts are set on pilgrimage.*
*. . . They go from strength to strength,*
*till each appears before God in Zion.*
PSALM 84:5, 7 NIV

Pilgrims are people who go on long journeys, with God as their only destination. In a sense, our entire lives can be pilgrimages. Even though God is *always* with us, we perceive our life as a journey toward Him, with stopping places along the way. Again and again, God meets us anew—all the way to heaven.

## God's Promise

*"I'll stay with you, I'll protect you wherever you go. . . . I'll stick with you until I've done everything I promised you."*
GENESIS 28:15 MSG

We really can't hear it enough—God will stay with us! He's not going to get tired of us and walk away. He's not going to give up on us because we keep making stupid mistakes. He doesn't get bored or angry, and He's never inattentive or preoccupied with something else. There's no danger too big or too small for Him to handle. He'll stick with us for eternity!

## Homes and Hugs

. . . . . . . . . . . . . . . . . . . . . . . . . . . . . . .

*"The eternal God is a dwelling place,
and underneath are the everlasting arms."*

DEUTERONOMY 33:27 NASB

All of us need a home, a place where we feel we belong, a place of safety where we can let down our guards and rest. But no set of four walls will ever be as true a home as God's presence! All of us also need hugs from the people who love us. We need the comfort of being enveloped by love. But no human hug is as strong as God's.

# Glad Hearts

· · · · · · · · · · · · · · · · · · · · · · · · · · · · · · · · · · · ·

*You have. . .made him glad*
*with the joy of your presence.*
PSALM 21:6 NIV

The psalmist wasn't afraid to yell at God; the psalms are full of anger, rage even. They express the long-ago poet's despair, frustration, and resentment. But the psalmist also experienced the joy of living in God's presence. In between all those angry psalms, verse after verse assures us that our God is a joyful God, a God of gladness—and in His presence we too will be glad.

# Body and Soul

*But if the Spirit of Him who raised Jesus from the dead dwells in you, He who raised Christ Jesus from the dead will also give life to your mortal bodies through His Spirit who dwells in you.*

ROMANS 8:11 NASB

We already mentioned that the Living God lives inside us. This isn't only a spiritual promise. This verse from Paul's pen tells us that the Spirit of God—the same powerful Spirit who brought Jesus back to life—lives in our physical bodies. Our arms and legs, brains and lungs, hearts and intestines are all the dwelling place of God!

# Making God Visible

*No one has seen God at any time;*
*if we love one another, God abides*
*in us, and His love is perfected in us.*
1 JOHN 4:12 NASB

In this verse, John is describing the "angel of God's presence" that we spoke of earlier. Not only do others carry God's message of love to us in visible, tangible ways, but we too are called to be God's "angels," His ambassadors who carry His love into the world in all sorts of concrete ways. When we do, He is present with others—and He is present with us!

# The Helper

. . . . . . . . . . . . . . . . . . . . . . . . . . . . . . . . . . .

*"I will ask the Father, and He
will give you another Helper,
that He may be with you forever."*
JOHN 14:16 NASB

The disciples had the amazing privilege of Jesus'
physical presence. They walked with Him and talked
with Him. They knew His voice and the shape of His
hands. They saw His smile and looked into His eyes.
But then they faced an awful emptiness when He was
no longer physically with them. Jesus understood
how they were going to feel. He promised them—and
us—that though He can no longer be seen or touched,
His Spirit would never leave them.

## God's Love Songs

"The Lord your God is living among you. He is
a mighty savior. He will take delight in you with
gladness. With his love, he will calm all your fears.
He will rejoice over you with joyful songs."

ZEPHANIAH 3:17 NLT

On the darkest, dreariest days—those days when just
getting out of bed seems to take all your strength—
remember: God is there with you, living in the midst
of your life. You make Him happy, so happy that He's
singing you love songs. Let His love calm and comfort
your heart.

# *Learn It by Heart!*

. . . . . . . . . . . . . . . . . . . . . . . . . . . . . . . . . . . .

*"The Lord himself goes before you and will be
with you; he will never leave you nor forsake you.
Do not be afraid; do not be discouraged."*

DEUTERONOMY 31:8 NIV

Here's that same message again: "Do not be afraid!"
Learn this verse by heart. Repeat it whenever you feel
discouraged or anxious. Say it so many times that it
wears a groove in your mind and in your heart. . .
until you begin to truly believe that God will never
leave you.

# Both Far and Near

. . . . . . . . . . . . . . . . . . . . . . . . . . . . . . . .

*"Am I a God who is only close at hand?" says the
Lord. "No, I am far away at the same time. . . .
Am I not everywhere in all the heavens and earth?"*
JEREMIAH 23:23–24 NLT

Some people say God is too holy to be present in
the ordinary world, while others insist He is in nature,
in human faces, in our own minds and bodies. In this
verse, God says, "You're both right! I'm right here
with you—*and* I'm far too great to be contained by
your small world. But it doesn't matter. Far or near, I
am everywhere!"

# A Message from the Holy One

. . . . . . . . . . . . . . . . . . . . . . . . . . . . . . . .

*A Message from. . .God, who lives in Eternity, whose name is Holy: "I live in the high and holy places, but also with the low-spirited, the spirit-crushed."*
ISAIAH 57:15 MSG

The theological term for a God who lives high above our physical world is *transcendence*, while *immanence* is the word for a God who is present everywhere we turn. In this verse, God tells us again, "Yes, I'm high and holy—but not so high that I'll ever leave you, even when you're feeling sad and crushed by life."

# Glimpses of God

. . . . . . . . . . . . . . . . . . . . . . . . . . . . . . . . . . . . . .

*"'You will seek Me and find Me when
you search for Me with all your heart.'"*
JEREMIAH 29:13 NASB

If God's always there, why can't we feel Him? If
He's real, why doesn't He give us more proof of
His presence? People have asked these questions
for thousands of years. They're a part of human
experience. But here's the answer: the life of faith
wasn't meant to be easy. You have to give everything
you have inside you—and only *then* will you begin
to catch glimpses of God's presence, glimpses that
will make you seek Him even harder.

# *He's Not Far Away!*

· · · · · · · · · · · · · · · · · · · · · · · · · · · · ·

*"That they would seek God, if perhaps they
might grope for Him and find Him, though
He is not far from each one of us."*

ACTS 17:27 NASB

This verse comes from one of Paul's sermons,
preached to people who were not familiar with
the God of Israel. He was trying to put the God
he loved into terms they would understand. Paul is
acknowledging that seeking God feels like groping
around in the dark—and he's promising that even
though all we see is darkness, God is standing right
there next to us.

# Building a
# House for God

. . . . . . . . . . . . . . . . . . . . . . . . . . . . . . . .

*In him you too are being built*
*together to become a dwelling*
*in which God lives by his Spirit.*
EPHESIANS 2:22 NIV

This verse from one of Paul's letters hints at how we can become more aware of God's presence with us. The important word is *together*. Living in the presence of God is not something we do alone. In our relationships with others, in the love we express and receive, we are constantly building a place where God will live among us.

# Until the End of the World

I am with you always,
even unto the end of the world.

MATTHEW 28:20 KJV

These were Jesus' last words to His friends before He left them to return to His Father. The promise He made then to His followers is ours as well. Again and again, we need to remind ourselves and each other that we live in a world where Jesus is real. He lived among us—and He still does. He always will.

## Everywhere!

. . . . . . . . . . . . . . . . . . . . . . . . . . . . . . . . . . . . . . . .

*Where can I go from your Spirit? Where can I flee
from your presence? If I go up to the heavens, you
are there; if I make my bed in the depths, you are
there. If I rise on the wings of the dawn, if I settle
on the far side of the sea, even there your hand will
guide me, your right hand will hold me fast.*
PSALM 139:7–10 NIV

Is there any blessing greater than that expressed by
these verses?

# Part 9:
# BEING A BLESSING
# TO OTHERS

*Give More*

It is more blessed to
give than to receive.
ACTS 20:35 KJV

God not only wants to bless us, but He also wants us to bless others. In fact, He wants us to think more about giving blessings than we do about receiving blessings. But then something funny happens. When we stop asking for blessings and focus on giving, we'll get more blessings than we would have otherwise. It's one of those paradoxes of God's Kingdom, something that doesn't seem to makes sense—but is true.

# A Never-Ending Cycle

. . . . . . . . . . . . . . . . . . . . . . . . . . . . . . . .

*God who gives seed to the farmer that becomes*
*bread for your meals. . .gives you something you*
*can then give away, which grows into full-formed*
*lives, robust in God, wealthy in every way,*
*so that you can be generous in every way.*
2 CORINTHIANS 9:10–11 MSG

Here's that blessing circle again. The more we give, the more we're blessed. The more we're blessed, the more we have to give. It's like the water cycle, where water evaporates from the earth into the clouds, and the clouds rain water back to earth, a never-ending cycle of life and growth.

# True Treasure

. . . . . . . . . . . . . . . . . . . . . . . . . . . . . . . . . . . . .

*Do good. . .be rich in good works. . .*
*be generous and ready to share, storing up. . .*
*the treasure of a good foundation for the future, so*
*that they may take hold of that which is life indeed.*
1 TIMOTHY 6:18–19 NASB

This verse explains what real wealth means, as well as the real purpose of wealth. Doing good to others is what makes us truly rich—and it's all meant to be shared! Giving builds the foundation we need not only for our future lives but for life itself. No other treasure lasts.

# Blessing versus Cursing

"Bless those who curse you.
Pray for those who hurt you."
LUKE 6:28 NLT

As His followers, we should take Jesus' words to us very seriously, but we often don't. We feel justified when we complain about people who hurt us. We fume and brood over insults and slights. And it never occurs to us that this is sin, something that damages our relationship with God. We don't realize that we're cursing rather than blessing. Jesus wants even our thoughts to be filled with blessings, not curses.

*Blessing Our Enemies*

. . . . . . . . . . . . . . . . . . . . . . . . . . . . . .

*If you see your enemy hungry,*
*go buy that person lunch,*
*or if he's thirsty, get him a drink.*
ROMANS 12:20–21 MSG

Not only are we to pray for the people who have hurt us, but we are also to bless them in visible, tangible ways. God asks us to look for opportunities to show them little kindnesses. He wants us to pay attention to what they need, to look for chances to help them in any way we can. This business of blessing our enemies is serious stuff!

# *Channels of Blessing*

* * * * * * * * * * * * * * * * * * * * * * * * * * * * *

*"I will save you, and you will be
a blessing. Do not be afraid,
but let your hands be strong."*
ZECHARIAH 8:13 NIV

Sometimes we may doubt our own abilities to be a blessing to others. We may feel we don't have anything to offer—or we think that whatever we could offer wouldn't be good enough. God asks us to take our eyes off our faults and inadequacy and simply get busy, our eyes on Him. When we open our hearts and lives, His strength and love can flow through us, out into the world, blessing everyone it touches.

# Called

Be harmonious. . .kindhearted, and humble in spirit;
not returning evil for evil or insult for insult, but
giving a blessing instead; for you were called for
the very purpose that you might inherit a blessing.
1 PETER 3:8–9 NASB

We may tell ourselves, "Of course, I know that, I do that." But do we? This is a way of living that's radically different from our customary attitudes and actions. It doesn't leave room for complaining and gossiping. As individuals, we may be called to do many things, but this is the overarching vocation we all share—to bless others with our words, thoughts, and actions.

## Bonus and Blessing

. . . . . . . . . . . . . . . . . . . . . . . . . . . . . . . . .

*"Give away your life; you'll find life
given back, but not merely given back—
given back with bonus and blessing."*
LUKE 6:38 MSG

Here again Jesus is talking about the blessing circle, that nonsensical Kingdom paradox. Give away your very life—because that's the only way you'll have a real life. Give away absolutely everything you have, every thought and thing, every emotion and action—and you'll still never be able to give as much as God gives back to you.

## Behind the Scenes

. . . . . . . . . . . . . . . . . . . . . . . . .

*"When you do something for someone else,
don't call attention to yourself. You've seen
them in action, I'm sure—'playactors' I call
them. . .acting compassionate as long as someone
is watching, playing to the crowds. They get
applause, true, but that's all they get. When you
help someone out, don't think about how it looks.
Just do it—quietly and unobtrusively. That is the
way your God, who conceived you in love,
working behind the scenes, helps you out."*
MATTHEW 6:2–4 MSG

Here's how Jesus wants us to bless others—humbly,
lovingly, with no focus on ourselves.

# Sowing Peace

. . . . . . . . . . . . . . . . . . . . . . . . . . . . . . . . . . .

*Peacemakers who sow in peace*
*reap a harvest of righteousness.*
JAMES 3:18 NIV

One of the ways we bless others is by working to create peace in the world around us. Some of us may be called to take large actions, to write letters and books, make speeches or run for office—but we're all called to build peace in our individual lives in small, tangible ways every single day. In each relationship, each interaction with another (no matter how casual), God asks us to bless the world with His peace and love.

# Part 10:
# THE BLESSING OF
# ETERNAL LIFE

*Abundant Life*

*I am come that they might
have life, and that they might
have it more abundantly.*
JOHN 10:10 KJV

We've talked about many kinds of blessings. In the end, all those blessings, both spiritual and material, can be contained in the blessing Jesus is talking about here—abundant life. Eternal life doesn't merely go on forever. It's a life that has no limits, not in time, not in strength, not in love. It's a life that's deep and rich, full of countless blessings.

## Life Forevermore

The LORD bestows his blessing,
even life forevermore.
PSALM 133:3 NIV

Most of us have a vague idea about eternity, an unknown realm beyond death, far off in the future. But the psalmist is speaking in the present tense. Eternal life starts now. The Hebrew word for this life—*chayah*—has a breadth of meaning: to come to life in a new way; to be restored to life after being dead; to be healed; to be kept alive; to be nourished; to recover from illness. And it's all happening *right now*. We don't have to wait until we die!

# Healed

. . . . . . . . . . . . . . . . . . . . . . . . . . . . . .

*Store my commands in your heart.*
*If you do this, you will live many years,*
*and your life will be satisfying.*
PROVERBS 3:1–2 NLT

Think about scripture. Dwell on it. Commit it to memory. Fill your mind with it. It will do you good. It will give you life! The Hebrew word that's been translated as *life* and *live* implies being restored to life after a serious illness. It's the sort of life that is so full, so healthy, that it really can't be measured in years. Hear God's words and you too will experience this life.

## Blessings Forever

*You will make known to me the path of life; in Your presence is fullness of joy; in Your right hand there are pleasures forever.*

PSALM 16:11 NASB

This verse mentions blessings we've already discussed—God's guidance, His joy, His presence—but it adds another element to them all: *forever.* Here's how *Strong's Concordance* explains what the psalmist meant when he used that word: "The bright goal in the distance that's travelled toward; splendor, confidence, victory that is perpetual, constant and ongoing." In other words, all of this exists at the end of our journeys on earth. It's also constantly there, right now.

# The Water of Life

. . . . . . . . . . . . . . . . . . . . . . . . . . . . . . .

*The water that I shall give him*
*shall be in him a well of water*
*springing up into everlasting life.*
JOHN 4:14 KJV

In the New Testament, the Greek word used for "life" is *zoé. HELPS* Word-Studies gives this definition for how Jesus is using the word: "physical and spiritual life, all life throughout the universe, which always and only comes from and is sustained by God's self-existent life. The Lord intimately shares His gift of life with people, creating each in His image which gives all the capacity to know His eternal life."

# The Joyful Path of Life

*"You have shown me the way
of life, and you will fill me
with the joy of your presence."*
ACTS 2:28 NLT

The blessing of eternal life can't be separated from the blessing of God's presence. It can't be separated from His joy either, and the blessing of His guidance is wrapped up in it too. Eternal life is our destination, but it's also a path, a path filled with joy, a path we're walking right now, led each step of the way by God's presence with us.

*Life beyond Time*

"*I am the resurrection and the life.
Anyone who believes in me
will live, even after dying.*"
JOHN 11:25 NLT

When we look at the Greek words in this verse, we find that Jesus is talking about a life that is both inside and outside time. *HELPS* Word-Studies says that it is what gives time its "everlasting meaning" even while it's also "time-independent." It "does not focus on the future *per se*, but rather on the *quality*." Eternal life is "right now, experiencing this *quality of God's life* now as a present possession." That's a pretty amazing blessing!

## Changed Priorities

. . . . . . . . . . . . . . . . . . . . . . . . . . . . . . . . . . . .

*"Don't be so concerned about perishable things like food. Spend your energy seeking the eternal life that the Son of Man can give you."*

JOHN 6:27 NLT

If we could just remember that we live both inside and outside time, in the same eternal realm with Jesus, we'd stop worrying so much about whether we'll have enough in this world. Our perspective would shift; our priorities would change. We'd live in the stream of never-ending blessing that is God's life, our eyes fixed on Jesus.

# Leaving It All

. . . . . . . . . . . . . . . . . . . . . . . . . . . . . . . . . .

*"And everyone who has left houses or brothers
or sisters or father or mother or children or farms
for My name's sake, will receive many times
as much, and will inherit eternal life."*
MATTHEW 19:29 NASB

God calls us to live in loving relationship with others—
and yet when Jesus talks like this, He sounds as though
He's saying the exact opposite, as though He wants us
to abandon our children and our parents, our homes
and our work. What He's really talking about though,
is the absolute surrender of giving everything we love
to Him. We're no longer in control. He is.

## Missing the Target

*Those who live only to satisfy their own sinful nature will harvest decay and death from that sinful nature. But those who live to please the Spirit will harvest everlasting life from the Spirit.*

GALATIANS 6:8 NLT

The Greek concept for sin is very simple. It means simply "failing to hit the mark." When we let our selfish egos run the show, we are like arrows that miss their target. Our target is life—but unless we surrender our egos to the Spirit, our arrows are all hitting death instead. It's as simple as that.

# Surprise!

. . . . . . . . . . . . . . . . . . . . . . . . . . . . . . . . .

*Now that you've found you don't have to listen to
sin tell you what to do. . .what a surprise! A whole,
healed, put-together life right now, with more and
more of life on the way! . . . God's gift is real life,
eternal life, delivered by Jesus, our Master.*
ROMANS 6:22–23 MSG

We have a choice; we don't have to keep shooting
our arrows in the wrong direction! When we choose
to aim toward God, our lives are changed in the
here and now: they're made whole, all their broken
places mended. . .and new life, new blessings keep
on coming.

# John 3:16

. . . . . . . . . . . . . . . . . . . . . . . . . . . . . . . . . . . . . . .

*For God so loved the world,*
*that he gave his only begotten Son,*
*that whosoever believeth in him should*
*not perish, but have everlasting life.*
JOHN 3:16 KJV

If you grew up going to Sunday school, you probably know this verse by heart. The words may have become *too* familiar, so take a moment to think about what this verse really means. It's the message of the Gospel all wrapped up in a nutshell: God loves you. . .God gives you His Son. . .through Jesus you have life. . . in Him you'll never die.

# The Shadow of Death

- - - - - - - - - - - - - - - - - - - - - - - - - - - - - - -

*"The people living in darkness have seen a
great light; on those living in the land of the
shadow of death a light has dawned."*
MATTHEW 4:16 NIV

Death is the great mystery, the dark unknown that
shadows all life. For us, death means sorrow. It means
losing the people we love. For us, it may mean fear,
even terror. And there's no escaping it. Everyone we
love will die, and our dying day will come to each one
of us. But Jesus let us know that death is not the end.
Night may fall—but a new dawn will come.

## Blessings Now

The LORD shall increase you more
and more, you and your children.
PSALM 115:14 KJV

Eternal life waits for us on the other side of death—but
it also expands our lives right now. It makes them fuller,
wider, deeper. It gives us more life than we ever knew
was possible. And this promise of eternal blessing
isn't only ours. It's so big that it spreads out from us.
It reaches our children too. The Lord's blessings have
no limits.

## Good Things

*Every good gift and every perfect*
*gift is from above, and cometh*
*down from the Father of lights.*
JAMES 1:17 KJV

Somewhere along the way, quite a few Christians got the idea that anything we enjoy is a temptation to sin. And it's true: anything we put ahead of God can become our little-g god. But that doesn't mean the things we like most are sin in and of themselves. All the good things in our lives come directly from God. They're a part of the eternal life He's blessed us with right now.

## Everlasting Love

. . . . . . . . . . . . . . . . . . . . . . . . . . . . . . . .

*"I have loved you, my people, with an
everlasting love. With unfailing love
I have drawn you to myself."*
JEREMIAH 31:3 NLT

God's love never ends. It never fails. It's unconditional.
It's broader and deeper than anything we could ever
comprehend, because it has no limits, no boundary
lines it refuses to cross. Wherever we go, it follows us.
It pulls at our hearts, because somewhere inside us all,
we know God's love is the source of all our joy. God's
everlasting love isn't a part of eternity. It *is* eternity.

## Abundant Blessing

...........................................

*From his abundance we have all received*
*one gracious blessing after another.*
JOHN 1:16 NLT

God can give us abundant blessings because He Himself is rich with abundance. When we enter into a relationship with God, we experience His endless wealth. We become aware that we live in a stream of blessing that never ends. God's blessings will carry us all our lives—and they will carry us through death and into the world beyond.

# Unfolding God's Tablecloth

*Not a day goes by without
his unfolding grace.*
2 CORINTHIANS 4:16 MSG

Imagine a tablecloth folded tightly into a small square, only a few inches across. As you start to unfold it, however, you realize it's not small at all; it's actually long and wide. The more you unfold it, the longer and wider it becomes. God's blessings are like that: not a day goes by that He's not unfolding new expressions of His grace in your life. His tablecloth of blessing is longer and wider than anything you can imagine!

# Fruit Trees

. . . . . . . . . . . . . . . . . . . . . . . . . . . . . . . .

*Blessed is the one. . .whose delight is in the law
of the LORD. . . . That person is like a tree planted
by streams of water, which yields its fruit in
season and whose leaf does not wither.*
PSALM 1:1–3 NIV

When God gives us the blessing of His life, we thrive.
We put down strong roots. God's life flows into us,
the way trees pull water up from the earth into their
branches and leaves. Even though we experience all
the effects of this world's time, eternity keeps us green.
Our lives are rich and fruitful.

## God's Forever House

. . . . . . . . . . . . . . . . . . . . . . . . . . . . . . . .

*Surely your goodness and unfailing love*
*will pursue me all the days of my life,*
*and I will live in the house of the LORD forever.*
PSALM 23:6 NLT

When my mother taught me this psalm long ago, it was one of her greatest gifts to me. In every difficult moment of my life, I repeat it. Its words ran through my head as I sat by my mother's deathbed—and I knew she was already living in the Lord's house, and she always would. God's love is always chasing us, always welcoming us, even in the valley of the shadow of death.

# Keys to the Kingdom

. . . . . . . . . . . . . . . . . . . . . . . . . . . . . . . . . . . . .

*"It gives your Father great happiness
to give you the Kingdom."*
LUKE 12:32 NLT

Sometimes when we pray, we act as though God is a stingy, distant authority figure. We plead with Him to give us the things we need. We beg Him to bless us. But we don't need to pray like that. Instead, we can pray with confidence. We don't have to beg. It makes God happy to bless us. God's Kingdom is rich and full, immense and lovely—and He wants to give us the whole entire thing!

# *Heart's Desire*

. . . . . . . . . . . . . . . . . . . . . . . . . . . . . . . . . . . . . . .

*Take delight in the Lord, and he will*
*give you the desires of your heart.*
PSALM 37:4 NIV

Sometimes it feels as though we have an empty place inside us that can never be filled, no matter how many things we get. That empty place is real, but material possessions can never fill it up. The Bible says that God put eternity into our hearts. Deep inside our innermost beings we yearn for all that eternity holds, all its abundance and beauty. Only God can give us the deepest, real desires of our hearts.

# God's Plans

*"For I know the plans I have for you,"
declares the LORD, "plans to prosper
you and not to harm you, plans to
give you hope and a future."*
JEREMIAH 29:11 NIV

The future scares us sometimes. We can't predict what sorrows and loss lie ahead. On the other hand, we *can* predict some of the losses that will come—like aging and the eventual deaths of those we love—and that's almost worse! But we don't need to live in fear. Instead, we can read and reread this verse! No matter what this world tells us, God always keeps His promises.

# Praise Song

. . . . . . . . . . . . . . . . . . . . . . . . . . . . . . . . . . . .

*Let all that I am praise the LORD; may I never forget*
*the good things he does for me. He forgives all my*
*sins and heals all my diseases. He redeems me from*
*death and crowns me with love and tender mercies.*
*He fills my life with good things.*
PSALM 103:2–5 NLT

Since all these eternal blessings are ours, our entire
being should sing with praise!

## *Stay Connected*

*"Your Father knows exactly what
you need even before you ask him!"*
MATTHEW 6:8 NLT

We need to pray. The Bible tells us to "pray without ceasing" (1 Thessalonians 5:17 KJV). But we don't pray because God needs to be told what we need. We pray because we need to be in vital connection with God; we need to be always aware that we are living in eternity. God already knows what we need, better than we do ourselves. We don't need to give directions as to how He should bless us!

# Richness of Life

............................................

*The blessing of the LORD*
*makes a person rich.*
PROVERBS 10:22 NLT

The Hebrew word used here for "makes rich" is *ashar*, which means "creates abundance." When we talk about blessing, that's what we really mean—the abundant riches, thriving health, overflowing bounty that God pours into our lives in countless shapes and forms, myriad varieties, all the depth and width that's contained in eternity. This richness of life is what God's blessings create for us and in us. This is the life we enter into through Jesus.

# God's Nature

· · · · · · · · · · · · · · · · · · · · · · · · · · · · · · · · · · ·

*Surely you have granted
him unending blessings.*
PSALM 21:6 NIV

*Unending.* The Bible uses that word over and over, telling us again and again that eternity and blessing are part of God's very nature. His being has no end, no limits. And since God is love (1 John 4:8), His love is constantly flowing around us and into us—an unending stream of blessings.

# God's Faithful Love

. . . . . . . . . . . . . . . . . . . . . . . . . . . . . . . . . . . . . . . . . .

*I cry out, "My splendor is gone! Everything I had hoped for from the LORD is lost!" The thought of my suffering. . .is bitter beyond words. I will never forget this awful time, as I grieve over my loss. Yet I still dare to hope when I remember this: The faithful love of the LORD never ends! His mercies never cease.*

LAMENTATIONS 3:18–22 NLT

God's blessing isn't like an eternal raincoat that protects us from sorrow. Awful times will come. We will grieve over losses. And yet, even then, we can be confident that God's love is faithful. We live in eternity—and God is still blessing us.

## God's Blessing

*If you listen obediently to the Voice of GOD. . .GOD, your God, will place you on high. . . . All these blessings will come down on you and spread out beyond you because you have responded to the Voice of GOD, your God: GOD's blessing inside the city, GOD's blessing in the country; GOD's blessing on your children, the crops of your land, the young of your livestock, the calves of your herds, the lambs of your flocks. GOD's blessing on your basket and bread bowl; GOD's blessing in your coming in, GOD's blessing in your going out.*

DEUTERONOMY 28:1–6 MSG

All those blessings are yours. God has promised!

# Expanded Editions of *The Bible Promise Book®* Just for Women

## *The Bible Promise Book® for Women— Prayer and Praise Edition*

Now available in a deluxe, expanded *Prayer and Praise Edition* for women featuring the beloved King James Version of the Bible plus encouraging prayers and inspiring hymn lyrics. With dozens of relevant topics—including Comfort, Faith, Hope, Joy, Love—women will find hundreds of verses included.

DiCarta / 978-1-62836-645-7 / $14.99

## *The Bible Promise Book® for Women— Prayer Edition Journal*

This delightful journal fits perfectly into a woman's prayer life. Featuring scripture, encouraging prayers, inspiring quotes, and generous journaling space, women of all ages won't be able to resist this lovely package. Journalers will find themselves encouraged and inspired to record all of the ways they are blessed and loved by their heavenly Father.

DiCarta / 978-1-63409-075-9 / $16.99